Pine Trees

By Allan Fowler

Consultants
Martha Walsh, Reading Specialist

Jan Jenner, Ph.D.

Children's Press®
A Division of Scholastic Inc.
New York Toronto London Auckland Sydney
Mexico City New Delhi Hong Kong
Danbury, Connecticut

Designer: Herman Adler Design
Photo Researcher: Caroline Anderson
The photo on the cover shows conifers growing in Bridger National Forest,
Wyoming.

Library of Congress Cataloging-in-Publication Data

Fowler, Allan.
    Pine trees / by Allan Fowler.
      p. cm. — (Rookie read–about science)
    Includes index.
    Summary: This introductory book discusses needles, cones, and the
different kinds of pine trees.
    ISBN 0-516-21685-6 (lib. bdg.)   0-516-25987-3 (pbk.)
    1. Pine—Juvenile literature. [1. Pine. 2. Trees.] I. Title. II. Series.
QK494.5.P66 F68 2001
585'.2—dc21

                                       00-055571

GROLIER
PUBLISHING
1 2 3 4 5 6 7 8 9 10 R 10 09 08 07 06 05 04 03 02 01

Why are pine trees special?

Ponderosa pines

Pine trees are evergreens. That means they are always green. The leaves of some trees, such as maple trees, change color in the fall.

But pine trees stay green
all year long.

needle

The leaves of a pine
tree are thin and sharp.
They are called needles.

Pine trees store water
in their needles.

On most pine trees, needles grow in clusters, or groups.

There are two, three, or five needles in each cluster.

cluster ———>

Many trees grow flowers or fruit. But pine trees are conifers. They grow cones.

pinecone

Pinecones are woody
and bumpy. They come
in different shapes.

Pine trees reproduce,
or make more pine
trees, using cones.

Every pine tree has both
big and small cones. The
small cones are filled with
dusty bits called pollen.

pollen

Pollen travels in the wind.
If pollen lands inside a big
cone on another pine tree, a
seed may grow in the cone.

When this seed falls on good soil, a new pine tree will grow.

Alaska

You can find pine trees in many parts of the United States and Canada.

They grow as far north as Alaska, and as far south as Florida. Hillsides are often covered with pine trees.

Florida

There are different kinds of pine trees. They are used to make many things.

Cedar is a kind of pine tree. The wood in your pencil might be cedar.

White cedar

Cedar wood has a nice smell. It keeps insects away.

Many people keep their clothes in cedar trunks and cabinets.

White pines, ponderosa pines, and Douglas firs are timber trees. Timber is wood used for building things.

White pine logs

Some Douglas firs grow very tall. They can grow taller than a thirty-story building.

24

Other kinds of pine trees give us a gummy material called resin (REZ-in).

People use resin to make tar for paving roads.

People turn chips of wood from pine trees into a thick wet paste called pulp. They make paper out of pulp.

Wood chips

Pulp

Paper mill

The paper in the book
you are reading now might
have been a pine tree!

Eastern white pine

Words You Know

cedar

evergreens

needles

pinecones

30

pollen

pulp

tar

timber

31

Index

About the Author

Allan Fowler is a freelance writer with a background in advertising. Born in New York, he now lives in Chicago and enjoys traveling.

Photo Credits

Photographs ©: Dembinsky Photo Assoc.: 9, 29, (E.R. Degginger), 5, 30 top right (Terry Donnelly), 10, 11, 30 bottom right (Michael P. Gadomski), 17, 22, 31 bottom right (Bill Lea), cover (Scott T. Smith); Photo Researchers, NY: 27 bottom (Rosenfeld Images LTD/SPL), 14, 31 top left (Scott Camazine), 26 (Alan Carruthers), 23 (M.J. Griffith), 27 top, 31 top right (Tom Hollyman), 3 (Tom & Pat Leeson), 12 (Kathy Merrifield), 19, 30 top left (Lincoln Nutting); Photri: 20; The Image Works: 24, 31 bottom left (Sven Martson); Visuals Unlimited: 15 (Gerald & Buff Corsi), 7 (Bert Krages), 16 (P.K. Siminski), 4 (Mark S. Skalny), 6, 30 bottom left.